George Washington and the American Revolution

by Joanne Wachter

Table of Contents

Introduction

George Washington was a famous soldier. Washington was a general, or leader of soldiers. He was a general in the **American Revolution**.

George Washington helped start the **United States of America**. He was the first **president** of the United States.

Read to learn more about George Washington.

▲ George Washington

Words to Know

American Revolution

Continental Army

Declaration of Independence

George Washington

Great Britain

Patriots

president

United States of America

United States Constitution

Valley Forge

See the Glossary on page 30.

3

What Was Washington's Early Life Like?

George Washington was born in 1732. He was born in the colony of Virginia. Virginia was a British colony in North America.

George Washington grew up on a plantation. A plantation is a large farm.

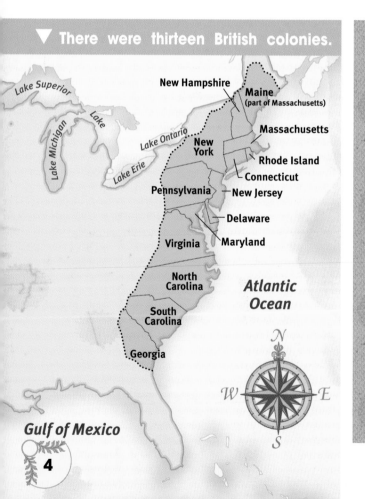

▼ There were thirteen British colonies.

Lake Superior
Lake Michigan
Lake
Lake Ontario
Lake Erie
New Hampshire
Maine (part of Massachusetts)
New York
Massachusetts
Rhode Island
Connecticut
Pennsylvania
New Jersey
Delaware
Virginia
Maryland
North Carolina
South Carolina
Georgia
Atlantic Ocean
Gulf of Mexico

Did You Know?

British means belonging to Great Britain.

Scotland
England
Wales

▲ Great Britain was the countries of England, Scotland, and Wales.

Washington was a surveyor. A surveyor measures land. A surveyor decides where boundaries should be. Boundaries show where property ends.

▲ George Washington was a surveyor.

Washington joined the British army in Virginia. He was a good soldier. He became a leader in the British army. He was only twenty-three years old.

▼ Washington was a leader in the British army.

British soldiers fought French soldiers
in North America. This was the French and
Indian War. Many Native Americans fought
in this war. They fought for the French soldiers.
Washington was a British soldier.

▼ **Washington fought in the French and Indian War.**

What Did Washington Do Before the American Revolution?

Washington left the British army in 1759. He became a farmer. He had a plantation in Virginia. The plantation was Mount Vernon.

Washington married. He married Martha Custis.

▼ Mount Vernon was Washington's home.

▲ Washington married Martha Custis.

Washington was a farmer. He made Mount Vernon a big plantation. He grew wheat and other crops.

It's a Fact

George Washington owned slaves. The slaves worked on his plantation.

▲ Slaves worked at Mount Vernon.

Learn More

Today, people still visit Mount Vernon. Go to: http://www.mountvernon.org/. Click on "museum tour."

Washington worked for the colony of Virginia. He was part of the Virginia government.

Washington believed **Great Britain** was not fair. He believed British taxes were not fair.

▲ Virginia had a government.

Other colonists believed Great Britain was not fair. Those colonists did not want to pay British taxes.

Those colonists were **Patriots**. The Patriots had a meeting. The Patriots wanted Great Britain to be fair. Washington went to the meeting.

▲ The meeting was the First Continental Congress.

11

The colonists and Great Britain began to fight. The first battles were near Boston.

▲ The colonists and the British fought near Boston.

The Patriots had another meeting. The Patriots wanted one big army. The army was for all the colonies. The army was the **Continental Army**. Washington was the leader of this army.

▲ Washington was the leader of the Continental Army.

What Did Washington Do During the American Revolution?

The British and the colonists fought. The war was the American Revolution. Washington was the leader of the colonists. Washington was a general.

The colonists were new soldiers. General Washington had to train the soldiers.

▲ General Washington was the leader of the soldiers.

General Washington's first battle was in Boston. Washington and his soldiers won. The British army left Boston.

It was 1776. British soldiers were in New York City. General Washington did not win in New York City. Washington and his soldiers went to New Jersey. Then, they went to Pennsylvania.

▲ **Washington and his soldiers won in Boston.**

 It's a
Fact

Patriots wrote the **Declaration of Independence** in 1776. The Patriots said the colonies were free from Great Britain. The Patriots said the colonies were the United States of America.

Chapter 3

German soldiers were in New Jersey. The German soldiers worked for the British army. Washington wanted the German soldiers to leave New Jersey.

Washington and his soldiers were in Pennsylvania. They crossed the river to New Jersey. They surprised sleeping German soldiers. Washington took the soldiers as prisoners. He took their supplies. Later, Washington won more battles in New Jersey.

▼ **Washington crossed the Delaware River.**

British soldiers were in Philadelphia. Washington and his soldiers fought the British soldiers. Washington did not win.

Washington and his soldiers stayed near Philadelphia. They stayed at **Valley Forge**.

▲ Washington and his soldiers went away from Philadelphia.

▲ Washington and his soldiers were cold.

The winter at Valley Forge was cold. The soldiers did not have much food. Many of the soldiers did not have shoes. The soldiers did not have warm clothes.

Many soldiers died because they needed food. Many soldiers died because they were sick.

Solve This

There were about 10,000 soldiers at Valley Forge. About $\frac{1}{4}$ of them died. About how many soldiers died?

Answer: About 2,500

The winter was difficult. The soldiers trusted General Washington. Most of the soldiers stayed with Washington.

People To Know

Friedrich Von Steuben was a German soldier. Friedrich Von Steuben trained Washington's soldiers. The soldiers became better fighters.

Von Steuben trained the ▶ soldiers at Valley Forge.

Washington and his soldiers fought many battles. They fought against the British soldiers. They fought for three years.

▲ Washington led his soldiers into battle.

Washington and his soldiers fought at Yorktown. Soldiers from France helped Washington. The British soldiers did not win the battle.

Great Britain and America had peace talks. Finally, in 1783 the war was over. The Americans won.

▲ **British soldiers lost the Battle of Yorktown.**

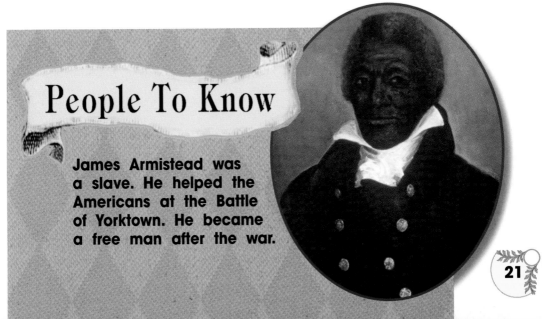

People To Know

James Armistead was a slave. He helped the Americans at the Battle of Yorktown. He became a free man after the war.

What Did Washington Do After the American Revolution?

The Americans won the American Revolution. The colonies were free from Great Britain. The colonies became one country. The country was the United States of America.

The United States of America needed laws. Men had a meeting to make the laws. George Washington was the leader of the meeting.

▲ **The meeting was the Constitutional Convention.**

The men wrote the **United States Constitution**. The Constitution is laws for the United States. The United States has the same Constitution today.

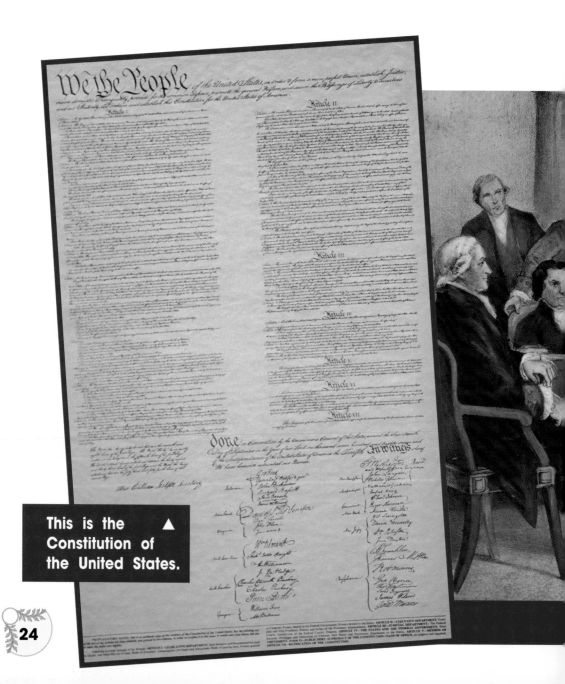

This is the ▲ Constitution of the United States.

One law was about the president. Leaders had to vote for the president.

The leaders voted for George Washington. Washington became the first president of the United States.

Did You Know?

Some people wanted George Washington to be a king. He said no.

▲ **Washington was the first president of the United States.**

Washington became president in 1789. The leaders voted for Washington a second time. Washington was president until 1797.

People wanted Washington to be president a third time. He said no.

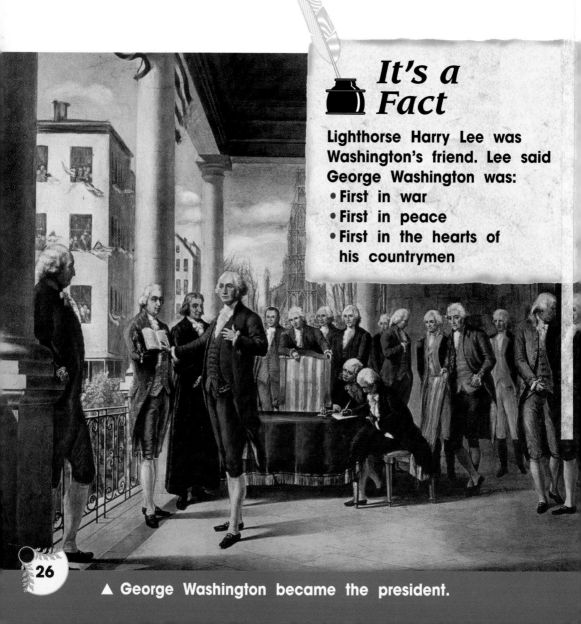

It's a Fact

Lighthorse Harry Lee was Washington's friend. Lee said George Washington was:
- First in war
- First in peace
- First in the hearts of his countrymen

▲ George Washington became the president.

Washington went back to Mount Vernon. He died on December 14, 1799.

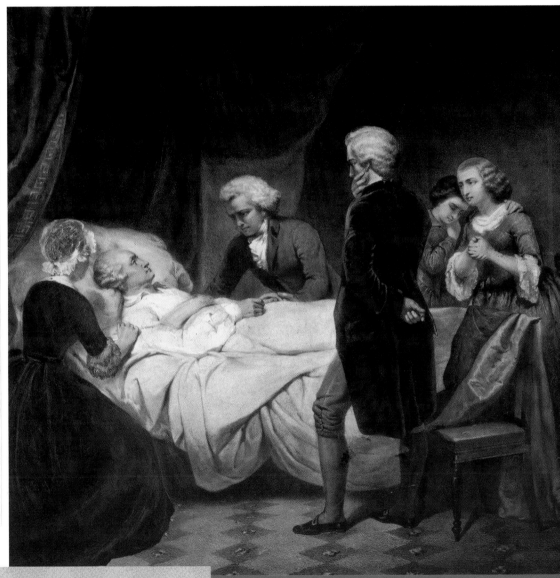

▲ Washington died at Mount Vernon.

Did You Know?

Many people called George Washington the father of his country.

Summary

George Washington was a leader in the American Revolution. Washington helped start the United States of America. Washington was the first president of the United States.

Time Line of George Washington's Life

1732
Washington was born.

1775
Washington became leader of the Continental Army.

Winter 1777–1778
Washington stayed at Valley Forge.

1758
Washington became a farmer at Mount Vernon.

1776
Washington had his first battle with British soldiers.

1781
Washington won the Battle of Yorktown. Yorktown was the last important battle of the American Revolution.

1789
Washington became the first president of the United States.

Think About It

1. Lighthorse Harry Lee said Washington was
   - First in war
   - First in peace
   - First in the hearts of his countrymen

   Why did Lee say this?
2. Why do people call Washington the father of his country?

1787
Washington was leader of the Constitutional Convention.

1799
Washington died.

Glossary

American Revolution war between America and Great Britain

George Washington fought in the **American Revolution**.

Continental Army the American army in the American Revolution

George Washington was the leader of the **Continental Army**.

Declaration of Independence paper saying the United States of America was a new, free country

George Washington did not sign the **Declaration of Independence**.

George Washington leader of the Continental Army and first president of the United States

George Washington was born in 1732.

Great Britain the countries of England, Scotland, and Wales

The Patriots wanted **Great Britain** *to be fair.*

Patriots colonists who wanted to be free from Great Britain

George Washington was a Patriot.

30

president the leader of the United States of America

George Washington was the first president.

United States of America a free country in North America

*The **United States of America** became a country in 1776.*

United States Constitution a paper that is laws for the United States

*George Washington signed the **United States Constitution**.*

Valley Forge a place where Washington and his soldiers stayed

*Winter at **Valley Forge** was very cold.*

Index